MEMOIRS

OF A

FEMALE VAGRANT,

WRITTEN BY HERSELF.

WITH

ILLUSTRATIONS.

"One half of the world does not know how the other half lives."

ENGLISH PROVERB.

London:

SOLD BY J. BURDITT, 60, PATERNOSTER-ROW,

Printed by J. W. MORRIS, Dunstable.

1806.

TO

JOSEPH WILSON, ESQ.

HIGHBURY HILL,

ISLINGTON.*

Dear Sir,

ALTHOUGH, when you requested me to prepare Mary Saxby's papers for publication, you left the manner of doing it entirely to my decision; I wish, before committing them to the press, to acquaint you with the state in which they will be printed; if it appears to you unobjectionable; and, at the same time, to assign some reasons for hoping that your benevolent design in publishing her narrative, will not be disappointed in the result.

---

* This letter, which was written just before the annexed sheets were sent to the press, has been thought the most suitable introduction to their contents.

I have thought it best to retain the writer's phraseology wherever correction did not seem requisite for greater perspicuity and precision ; apprehending that her own "unvarnished tale" would be most satisfactory to the serious and candid reader. I have taken no other liberty with her narrative, than that of omitting a few passages, which appeared to me irrelevant to the leading subject, or liable to misconstruction. The remarks which occurred to me, as likely to supply acceptable illustration, to suggest needful caution, or to promote general utility, I have thrown into marginal notes.; so that nothing that is not her own, is introduced into the text, I preferred this method to that of collecting such observations together at the close of the narrative ; because I hoped that they might be more impressive in a closer connexion with the passages to which they relate.

The papers which I received from you, terminate abruptly at the death of her younger son. Her daughter Kezia, the only surviving offspring of her marriage, believes that she extended the narrative to a later period: but if the supposed sequel of it exists, it cannot now be found. Should it be discovered, advantage shall be taken of any subsequent occasion, to annex it to the present account. In the mean time, I have attempted to supply the deficiency, by a recital of the principal occurrences which the writer was concerned in during the last seven years of her life, from information which has been communicated to me by her daughter; the person to whose relief in necessity, you have assigned whatever profits may arise from the publication. I hope that this circumstance will tend to increase its circulation: especially since the poor woman deserves, as well as needs, the assistance that may be derived from it; having diligently attended on her mother throughout her last illness, and afterwards borne the charges of her funeral. She has also lately been deprived of her husband, Benjamin Ping, who is spoken of in the conclusion of the narrative.

The display which is here afforded, of the vices and miseries of a vagrant life, may prompt the active beneficence of the present age, to regard the wandering classes of the poor, with that attention which is needful for their relief and reformation. It will, I hope, excite some thankfulness to divine Providence, in the hearts of those who are mercifully exempted from the wants and temptations of so deplorable a state of society; and some concern to rescue them, if possible, from imminent, and otherwise irretrievable ruin. A ray of light is here thrown on the different shades of their obscure condition; from the vagabond huckster, down to the ballad singer, the beggar, and the gypsy. These outcasts are a reproach to our nation, a pest to the country, and too often a fatal snare to unsteady and unwary youth. Should the worthy members of the "Society for bettering the condition of the Poor," be induced, by this pamphlet, to extend their humane and patriotic care to these numerous bands of semi-savages dispersed amidst our highly civilised countrymen, I shall rejoice in the accomplishment of so important an object.

To those, however, who duly prize the blessings of Christianity, the facts which are here detailed, will be contemplated in a still more affecting point of view. They will regard them as so many trophies in honour of Him, who "came to seek and save that which was lost." They will consider the writer of this narrative, as a wandering sheep, whom the great and good Shepherd pursued far from the fold, and carried back to it rejoicing. They will figure to themselves the angels of God exulting in the repentance of so hopeless a sinner, and will esteem it a privilege to join in their hymns of praise. Happily, the leading subject of this pamphlet is far from being a solitary occasion of such joy. She even had it in her power to record several similar instances, within the limits of her personal knowledge.

If any person should open these pages with a disposition more resembling that of the Prodigal's elder brother, may a perusal of them become the means of dispelling injurious and baneful prejudices, and of exciting a due concern to share in that mercy which is here so signally displayed: necessary as it is for the salvation of every son and daughter of Adam; and free, to all who seek it while it may be found!

The most numerous and respectable tes-
timonies to the authenticity of this account,
might easily have been procured; but I
thought that they would be superfluous.
No person who is acquainted with *you*, or
with myself, will question it: and to others,
I apprehend, the internal evidence will appear sufficient. Almost all the persons
whose names are introduced, are yet living:
and delicacy alone has prevented me from
denoting them more plainly than by the
consonants of their names, which will in-
dicate them to all who can be interested in
the discovery. Few persons have been so
generally known, still fewer in a subordi-
nate sphere so much respected, as the writer of this narrative, in the northern part
of Buckinghamshire, and the borders of
Northamptonshire and Bedfordshire.

You committed to me many more of her
papers, consisting chiefly of her daily medi-
tations, in prose and humble rhymes, during the latter years of her life. Of these,
some, at least of the former description,
would probably be acceptable to serious
readers: but as the Narrative may be of use
to many who might have little taste for her

pious soliloquies; and especially as it is desirable, for the advantage of the poor, that it should be published in a cheap form; I can hardly recommend that any other of her papers should, in the first instance, be presented to the public.

I am, Dear Sir,

Your obliged friend and servant,

SAMUEL GREATHEED.

Newport-Pagnel,
February 1. 1806.

CONTENTS.

PART I.

MEMOIRS

OF

A FEMALE VAGRANT.

PART I.

From her birth, to her return to her father's house.

I was born in London, in the year 1738. My
mother dying when I was very young, and my
father going into the army, I was exposed to
distress, even in my infancy.* I was continually
removed from the charge of one relation to that
of another; in consequence, I verily believe,
chiefly of my own perverse temper; which, be-

---

* Her parents were named John and Susanna Hollowell. Her
mother died at the birth of a second child, which did not survive her.
Of her father's children by his second marriage, two sons are now
living, who practise his business, of silk-weaving. Through the hands
of one of these, Spire Hollowell, and of Kezia Ping, one of the
writer's daughters, her narrative is now communicated to the public.

B

cause I had no parent, scorned to be under the controul of any of my friends, even at that early period. What an awful instance of the depravity of our nature, and the desperate wickedness of the human heart, till changed by sovereign grace! Yet, notwithstanding my vileness, the Lord was pleased to appear for me, by inclining the hearts of my father's brother, and of his dear wife, (who are both, I trust, now in glory, and whose memories are still precious to me) to take care of and provide for me. Whilst I lived with this worthy couple, I went to the Rev. Mr. Whitefield's school, at the tabernacle, near Moorfields; where I got that little learning, which, to my grief and shame, I have too often been very proud of. Through the goodness and mercy of God I retain it to this day; which is wonderful, considering the many years that I wandered without a guide or teacher. May the Lord make me truly thankful, and deeply humble under my misimprovement of so valuable a blessing!

Whilst I was at this school, I was constantly taken to public worship; and I can remember having felt at times a sharp conviction of my offences; but, alas, it proved like the morning cloud or early dew, and too soon disappeared! I still retained a wicked and impetuous temper, as I well remember in one instance particularly. I had highly provoked my dear aunt; and she shut me in a dark place, and sent for an old man, who came to the door with a knife in his hand, thinking it necessary to intimidate me to submission : but so bold and daring was I, that, instead of crying for pardon, I caught hold of the knife, and cut my hand in a most shocking manner; so that they never durst try such experiments with me any more.*

Soon after this, my father came home from abroad, and lived in the same house with us, working at his trade, which was that of a silk-weaver. Having no other child, he was too fond of me; and at that time could hardly bear to see me chastised, even when I well deserved it. And, oh my soul, canst thou reflect with a degree of gratitude on the kindness and love of an earthly parent, and not pause a moment to contemplate the unbounded, unparalleled love, of our dear heavenly Father, not only in the best of all gifts, a precious Saviour, but also in bearing so long, and dealing so gently, with such a daring offender? Eternal praises to his name! he does not willingly grieve nor afflict the children of men ; but even when constrained, as it were, by our complicated offences, for the vindication of his own glory, to correct his rebellious creatures, he seems to do it with a reluctant hand : for, " when his strokes

---

* The menace of the knife was so grossly improper, that this part of the experiment was probably devised, not by her aunt, but by the man whose assistance she had judged requisite. The result shews the absurdity of threatening children with any punishment that should not be inflicted if they persist in the fault.

are felt," they are much " fewer than our crimes, and lighter than our guilt."*

At one time, when my aunt had been chastising me, my father hearing her, came down stairs much chagrined, and immediately hired a house at a small distance, and took me home with him. He had soon reason, however, to repent of his conduct: I was as sore a trial to him, as I had been to the rest of my friends; and (oh that I could write it with tears of due contrition!) I repeatedly found means to elope from him. In the first of my excursions, I got among some women of the town, who gave me liquor that quite intoxicated me; they then stripped me almost bare, and in this plight my poor father found me. He afterwards went in search of those who robbed me, but could never find them; so he was forced to put up with the loss of my clothes.

Shortly afterwards, a serious woman came to rent a room in our house; and she had not been there long, before my father became strongly attached to her. She seemed very fond of me; and as I was very apt at reading, and proud to be praised, I used frequently to read to her in the Pilgrim's Progress, and other good books. At length my father and she were married: but the very name of stepmother gave me such disgust, that I could not endure it; and therefore I was

---

* Watts, psalm ciii.

not very careful to please her. I determined on a second elopement, which I soon found means to effect: but my scheme proved abortive; for my father soon followed me, and found me in St. James's Park, where I went to see the grand fire-works played off, on peace being proclaimed.* I had promised myself much pleasure from the sight; but was disappointed, being forced home between my father and another man. And now my poor, dear, grieved parent, thought he would effectually humble my proud spirit. He shut me up in a lower room which faced the street, and chained me to the bed-post: the children I used to play with were permitted to look through the window, and mock and scoff at me; and I think that, for three days, I had no other food than a few dry crusts, soaked in some pot-liquor.

My father was, notwithstanding, too fond of me; and I believe that my mother-in-law wished me well: but the means they used were unsuitable to their purpose; for instead of humbling my proud, perverse spirit, this exasperated me to the highest degree. I determined on revenge, as I imputed all to my stepmother: and when I got my liberty, and was set to work at winding quills for my father, I tore the silk, and threw it away, although I knew that I should be punished for it. When my father found it out, he locked me up,

---

* Feb. 2. 1749, when she was in the eleventh year of her age.

B 2

again, and whipped me, till, I believe, he made me promise to act better. But he still used wrong methods; for when he let me out of the room, he fastened a log to my leg. I was obliged to hold it up when I went to play; and one of our neighbours having lost something, I was accused, because I was seen with my hand in my pocket-hole, which was only to hold up my log. This sensibly touched my proud nature; and I was now determined, at all events, upon a final escape.

When I got my liberty, I quickly found means to run away; for, soon after, my father sent me on an errand, and gave me a shilling, and a plate to hold what I was to purchase. Being careless about pleasing him, I lost my time in catching flies on the rails as I went along; but in the midst of my sport I lost the shilling, and whilst I stood crying and looking for it, I dropt the plate, and broke that. Now, I durst not think of returning, but ran farther and farther from home. Oh what a scene of distress, sorrow, and trouble, did I bring myself into by this unguarded action! For several nights that I staid in town, I was forced to creep under bulks, or any where, to hide myself from the watchmen; and as soon as day broke, I went into the markets, to pick up rotten apples, or cabbage-stalks; as I had nothing else to support nature. At length, I met with a girl, who I thought would prove a suitable companion to me. We agreed to go into the country together; and though neither of us knew where we were going, we set out, and travelled several days, without any other food than what the hedges afforded. My companion, not being so hardy, and perhaps not so wicked as I, soon returned, and I was left alone. How I lived, I cannot now remember; but soon after she was gone, there fell a very deep snow, and I had nearly perished with cold and hunger. I can recollect sitting in a black-smith's shop, and holding my feet in my hands, to get some warmth into them. One night, I crept under a hovel for shelter, and there came an old beggar-man to lie down; seeing a child by herself, he asked me where I came from? I forget what I told him: I fear some lie, which, to my shame, I was very guilty of, though so young. Poor as he was, he had pity on me; and gave me a piece of fat bacon, which I ate, without bread, as greedily as if it had been the finest food.

Here my memory fails, as to my means of subsistence for some time. I had many temptations to steal, but could not as yet break through my former convictions. For some time, I wandered solitarily; until I was in a dismal plight, for want of cleansing, as well as of food. Many a time, have I narrowly escaped being entirely ruined by wicked men: but as the Lord always gave me a strong aversion to the very name of a common prostitute, so he, and he alone, kept me from becoming one, even so early. All my vileness since then (for which I desire ever to lie in the dust before him, and for which, I trust, he hath given me true repentance) is only known to him and my own conscience; yet, blessed be his name, he kept me from ever becoming one of that base character; and to him may I be helped to ascribe all the glory!*

I now wandered from town to town, till I met with a poor travelling woman, who had three daughters: and though she was a very ignorant person, yet the Lord disposed her to take pity on me in my forlorn condition; for she washed, combed, and fed me, and took as much care of me as if I had been her own. In this poor state, I might have been very happy; as she was a tender, motherly woman, and would have taught me to get my bread honestly, had I been ruled by her. But here again, my proud, imperious temper, began to shew itself incapable of any restraint. Her youngest daughter was about my age, and with her I soon contracted an intimacy. As we both had pretty good voices, we agreed to go about together, singing ballads; and to this end we determined on separating from her

---

* These circumstances afford encouragement for diligent endeavours to impress religious truths early on the minds of children, notwithstanding the utmost degree of perverseness that may appear in them. The violence of this girl's temper, and the injudicious treatment which she had consequently experienced, seemed to have brought her already into the most desperate of situations: yet all could not wholly obliterate the good effects of the religious instruction which she had received while under the care of her pious aunt.

mother. Ah, did young, inexperienced persons, know what misery awaited them, by giving way to their own headstrong passions, and escaping from the restraint of their elders, surely they would not rush on their ruin, as they too frequently do! My new companion and I were fully resolved upon our plan; and, to my present grief and self-condemnation, we speedily found means to effect it.*

Being then wholly left to ourselves, without any one to controul us, we ran wherever our blind fancy led us, into all sorts of company, singing in alehouses, at feasts and fairs, for a few pence and a little drink. At length, we met with a gang of gypsies; some of whom played on the fiddle, and one, in particular, was an exceeding good dancer. This fascinated us so much, that we needed little entreaty to go with them to their camp, which contained several tents, with men, women, and children. At first they behaved well to us; and, I think, made us separate tents: and,

---

* This instance of depravity is aggravated, by the miseries which she had already suffered, by the deliverance from them with which she had, in the utmost extremity, been favoured; and by the maternal kindness she had received from the poor woman whose daughter she had now seduced to elope with her. No provocation appears to have been given to this measure, and every feeling of gratitude was outraged by it. It demonstrates the natural hardness of the human heart; the proneness of children to receive and retain bad impressions; the fatal effects of vicious habits; and the inefficacy of every motive not arising from religious principle, to recover from such a state, or to restrain from progress in sin.

during summer, we liked it very well. As I was comparatively a good scholar, and could do something with my needle, I was highly approved of, which pleased me much. I soon found that a male companion was designed for me; and as this was the same young man that had allured me by his dancing, (to my great shame I write it) I loved him too well; and as he promised me marriage, consented to co-habit with him; in which sinful state I continued more than a year. By this time I had acquired all the manners of the gypsies, could use their cant terms pretty fluently, and was every way like them, excepting in colour.

I was still promising myself that the man with whom I lived would marry me, when I found, by his behaviour, that his affections were alienated from me, and fixed on another woman. She was near of kin to him, and a married person. Such conduct, I have since learned, is not uncommon amongst these people:* but as I was young and inexperienced, it so grieved me, that it nearly cost me my life. I well remember wandering into a wood, with an intention to starve myself. I must soon have perished there for want, had not the Lord in his great mercy prevented it, by in-

---

* Such appears to be the conduct of mankind in general, unless restrained by the operation of salutary laws, established habits of decency, or religious principle. Yet it will be found, in the progress of the narrative, that this gang of gypsies was less depraved than others of that denomination.

clining my associates to seek after me. After a diligent search, they found me out, and forced me back to my companion, who was willing, and even eager to receive me, in the quality of a secondary wife, or servant to the other woman, who then lived with him. To this humiliation, I was determined not to submit; although I loved him almost to distraction. The poor young woman who came with me, actually lived in that state; and I believe had seldom a moment's peace, till she found means to escape. I took the first opportunity of doing so; but accomplished my design with some difficulty, being very narrowly watched.

I travelled as far as Dover in Kent, with very little to support me; stopping, at times, to ask for a bit of bread, to keep me from starving. When I reached the coast, I met with a woman who sung ballads, which was a profitable trade in those parts; and she took me into partnership, till we had some words, and separated. As I was not disposed to be extravagant, I had collected a little money, and now set up for myself. A vessel was, at this juncture, wrecked near Sandwich; and the cargo, consisting of checks and muslins, was sold cheap; which afforded opportunity to me, and many more, to get clothed for a trifle. Soon after this, having made myself clean and smart, I joined company with a decent woman, who had some small children. Her husband, to the best of my recollection, was gone abroad;

and I think that she sold hardware. We could get no lodging for our money, except in a barn; and I was young, and in that line of life which attracted the notice of men. Though it is now so long ago, I still reflect, with horror on the one hand, and gratitude on the other, on the imminent danger, in which a kind providence watched over and preserved me.* One day, whilst with her, I was singing, when some sailors fixed their eyes on me, and marked which way I went. We could get no lodging for our money, except in a barn : and in the night the sailors came after us, and asked my companion where I was. The poor woman, in a fright, told them I was not there : but they swore they would have me ; and accordingly searched till they found, and dragged me out, disregarding the cries and lamentations of the woman and her children. They forced me along with them : but either my cries, or those of the poor woman, alarmed the farmer, who sent his servants, with lights, and dogs, after the sailors. Some of them

---

* No person, I am persuaded, that knew the writer, will suspect her of any falsehood in this part of the narrative, or of any affectation in her manner of expression. In conversation, she avoided, with remarkable delicacy, to detail the more licentious parts of her life ; and spoke of them, in general, with marks of the sincerest contrition and self abasement. Vice, like virtue, has its distinct degrees. This girl was betrayed, by personal attachment, into unlawful cohabitation ; but she was not addicted to lewdness. The laudable efforts that are now made for the purpose of reclaiming common prostitutes, may be encouraged by the facts which are here recorded.

were known by their voices; but they could never be laid hold of. When they found themselves disappointed, they either pushed me into a pond, or forced me to run into it, to get out of their hands; I can only remember that I was found in that situation, half clothed, having been torn out of bed. Through mercy I was recovered, conveyed to the nearest house, and taken care of.

Soon afterwards, I happened to attract the notice of some gypsies, who travelled in that part of the country; and having, by some means found that I could speak their cant language, they insisted on my going along with them. Had I long remained with them, I should, in all probability, have fallen a victim to the laws of our country; as they lived wholly by rapine and plunder, stealing sheep, or any thing they could lay their hands on, or getting large sums of money from young inexperienced people, under a pretence of telling their fortune. A woman who was among them, told me, that she got a diamond ring of a sailor, in this manner. They are frequently obliged to flee the country, lest they should be brought to jutsice. One circumstance I remember, with shame and grief, in which I was an accomplice in their diabolical practices; and, had we been detected, we must have suffered. Oh the exceeding wonders of the patience and forbearance of a good and gracious God, to such a daring offender; that he should ever magnify his mercy, in snatching me as a brand from the burning;

c

whilst I have cause to fear my poor fellow-sinners have been left to perish in their guilt! May the Lord grant, as I humbly hope I have had much forgiven, that I may love much; and oh may my spared life be more and more devoted to his service!*

PART II.

From her return, to her marriage.

AFTER the unhappy transaction to which I have alluded, I escaped from these gypsies, and got an honester employment, in weeding corn. Here I might have done pretty well, had it not been for a calamity. As I was at work, I felt a pain in the bend of my arm, which soon swelled and turned black, quite up to my shoulder; having apparently by some means received poison: and, as I had no friends, I could get little help; but I sold what few things I had, and at last was

---

* It surely implies some gross defect, either in the theory or the practice of our laws, that in a country so highly civilised as England, any part of the community should be suffered to remain in such a condition as that of the Gypsies.—The immediate subject of this narrative appears here to have approached the extreme of depravity, by falling into connexion with them. The slight impression which she still retained from a religious education, seems to have prevented her farther progress in wickedness, although it was inadequate to restore her to the paths of virtue.

forced to bow my stubborn spirit, and go to my father, in a poor plight. As he could not conveniently have me at home, on account of his family, for he had three or four children by his second wife, he took a room for me near him, and engaged a surgeon to attend me. They, doubtless, did what they could, but to no purpose. My poor father was at last obliged to clothe me, and get me into a hospital; where I remained almost all the summer. I went through various operations, and endured great pain; and had it not been for one of the surgeons, I must probably have had my arm cut off: but he was desirous of trying what could be done; and, through mercy, made a sound cure of it. But oh, how did I requite my poor parent! Instead of going home, to return thanks for his love to, and care over me, I set out and went into Kent, to pick hops; and I think it was there that I first saw the man, who, long afterwards, became my husband. Out of Kent, I went into Essex; where they would not suffer any one to travel without a licence, except they could give a very good account of themselves. I, not knowing the rules of the country, sung ballads in Epping market. In the course of the day, I became acquainted with a middle-aged woman, who looked like a traveller; and we went to sleep together at an alehouse. For this I soon smarted; as she proved to be a common woman, though I did not know it. Being in her company, and having been seen with her in the market, the constable came in the night, obliged us to leave our bed, and secured us till morning; when we were taken before a justice, who committed us both to Bride-well, ordering us both to be repeatedly whipped.* The keeper heard my story very candidly; and I believe he was a good man. Observing my youth and inexperience, he pitied me; and remonstrat-ed with the woman for drawing me into a snare. We were to be confined there six weeks, without any allowance. She was a good spinner; and he made her work, and give me half her earnings. As to being whipped, I knew little but the shame of it; for he took care not to hurt me. He lent me good books, gave me good counsel, and was very tender to me. I remember feeling some serious emotions, whilst reading, and some faint desires to improve by what I read and suffered; for my misery was extreme, from cold and hun-ger: but my heart being unchanged, as soon as I was set at liberty I returned to my former courses, wandering from place to place.

---

* While vigilance to prevent the practice of vagrancy is highly commendable, it should evidently be directed to the restraint and reformation of the unhappy individuals. It does not appear that either of these women was proved to have been guilty of any crime at Epping; and if so, neither of them ought to have been subjected to corporal punishment. In most cases, indeed, it tends rather to harden, than to reform criminals, especially females. Their confinement, and obligation to labour, might otherwise have been beneficial.

At length I met with my old companion, the gypsy with whom I had cohabited; and he again got me into his company. While my clothes lasted, they used me well: but they soon took them from me; and then kept me, as it were, in a state of slavery, and would by no means suffer me to go from them. But the man whom I had met with in Kent, finding out my situation, came and demanded me; and as the gypsy with whom I lived refused to part with me, the other, being a strong daring man, challenged him to fight for me, conquered him, and took me away in triumph. Here I only exchanged one state of slavery for another: for his mother and sister, though common travellers, thought me not good enough for him, and led us both a very unhappy life; though I did not then cohabit with him, and thought I never would, till we could be married, only remaining with them for company. I wished many times to have quitted them; but he never would suffer it, always saying he would marry me in spite of them. To my grief and shame I confess it, notwithstanding all my resolutions, I became pregnant by him: and what to do I knew not; especially as, when the season of haymaking came on, they insisted on his leaving me, to get employment in another part of the country. I was left with his mother, who promised to bring me after him when I should be delivered. Her daughter accompanied her brother: and after she was gone, I believe their mother would have been

c 2

a friend to me, had she not been so much given
to drinking, that I was obliged to help her, instead of receiving assistance from her.   I therefore took up my old trade of ballad-singing, and
soon got plenty of good clothes for myself and
my infant ; and saved a little money to carry us
into the hay country. I was delivered at Woburn,
in Bedfordshire, where I staid but a fortnight, as
I longed to see the father of my poor child, and
hoped he would soon make me his wife.   As his
mother knew where he worked, we travelled as
fast as my strength would permit, till we got near
the place, and heard, as we thought, his voice in
the hay-field. His mother went to call him ;
but oh, what a disappointment did I meet with
when she returned !   Her knees smote together ;
and she, pale as death, told me that her child was
gone for a soldier. The sister said that it was all
through me ; and both of them deserted me, and
even wronged me of what was my lawful right.

Destitute, helpless, and forlorn, I knew not
what course to take ; a poor fatherless baby at my
breast, my money gone, and in a strange place :
but here the Lord appeared for me, though I
knew him not. A poor woman that worked in
the field, seeing me so ill used, said she would
take care of me, till I could provide for myself.
When my case was made known, I found many
benefactors, who gave me money and clothes for
my child.   I promised the good woman who had
been so kind to me, to go into Kent with her to

pick hops; but this proved a snare to me. She was a very clean, sober, decent woman; and had one son, who was a clever youth. I took a great liking to her, and had reason to think her son became attached to me, though I do not remember that he discovered it for some time. When he did, I made strong objections, on account of my poor child, whom I wished never to have a stepfather. Soon afterwards I forsook their company: but the young man, knowing where I used to travel, followed me; and, in Woburn-park, absolutely swore he would kill me, if I did not promise to have him; and I know not how I escaped. After this I was informed, that he told his mother, if I would not live with him, he would go for a soldier; and she was so distressed at this, having no other son, that she declared, if he did, she would first kill me, and then herself.* This so intimidated me, that I knew not what to do. However, by some means, they got me again into their company; and reasoned with me on the absurdity of waiting for one who took no notice of me and my child. His letters to me were always intercepted; and on this account I was the more easily persuaded to cohabit with one whom I

---

* Several instances of such threats occur in this narrative, and there seems little room to apprehend that they would not have been fulfilled. A wandering life affords opportunities of eluding the effect of laws, while it tends to eradicate social affections, and to preclude religious instruction. The vagrant classes of the British poor appear to be inferior in civilization to the Bedouin Arabs.

believed to love me and my infant, of which his mother was remarkably fond. Still I refused to marry him, lest he should use the child ill afterwards; and as it was not then customary for travellers to marry, I saw no evil in it.* Since then, I hope the Lord hath truly humbled me for this and all my sins.

We soon had information that the father of my child was coming on furlough from his regiment; and knowing him to be a resolute desperate man, we were afraid to meet him. If we had removed together, he would probably have pursued and discovered us : ' my companion was therefore obliged to leave me with his mother, till the other might go back to his regiment. He came, as expected; and presently found us out. After a short time, he-insisted on my walking with him; which I did not dare to refuse. Though stung with guilt, yet I thought I had enough to reproach him with, and to excuse my own conduct. After some altercation, and mutual upbraiding, he told me that as he knew I had been used so ill by his sister, he would freely forgive all that was past, on condition that I would promise to leave the other man; and wait for him till his time was up (which he hoped would not

---

* It is to be feared, that the higher, as the lower classes of society among us, often make *custom*, instead of the divine commands, the criterion of right and wrong; and pay little regard to the approbation of God, if they can escape the censure of fellow creatures,

be long) when he would marry me: but (as we we were walking by a river-side) he swore, that if I refused to promise this, he would throw me in, and dispatch me at once. I believe that I promised; and I again joined company with his mother; his sister having gone, since I had parted with them, to cohabit with a man that had a wife and children. Thus she who had treated me with so much contempt, fell herself into a still greater snare: but I hope that the Lord gave her true repentance; for I had the pleasure to hear afterwards, that she had broken that connexion, and associated with the Methodists. The other young man went to London, and died there, of the small-pox; and I have good ground to believe that his mother became a serious christian; for, when she heard I was converted from my sinful course, she came to see me, and nursed me, when lying in; and we had some sweet conversation together. Oh that we may all meet around the throne of everlasting mercy! I have been particular respecting these things, to shew the goodness of God in preserving my worthless life, when exposed to imminent dangers; and in snatching one and another of my old companions in sin and iniquity, as brands from the burning.*

---

* These facts afford considerable encouragement to benevolent efforts for the temporal and spiritual recovery of the most profligate poor; and may teach the vilest characters among them not to abandon themselves to despair. They intimate also, what is illustrated in

John Saxby, the father of my child, soon came home, as his regiment was disembodied. He took me from his mother, and said that we should be married, as soon as we had a convenient opportunity. This, however, did not soon occur: for sometimes we abode at places where the clergy refused to marry travellers; and at other times, we had not money enough to discharge the expense. I am sorry to say, that this continued to be our state, till I had two more children. At length, I began to see the evil of it; and insisted on separating, if we were not married. He did not promise to prove the best of husbands; but he was not willing to part with me: so, hearing that the Rev. Mr. N⸺, who was then Curate of Olney, would not object to marry us, we went there, and were married, Jan. 3. 1771. Oh what a day of dissipation and vanity was this! Though we had three small children, there was as much spent on this occasion as would have gone far toward clothing them.*

the progress of this narrative, that a plain and zealous ministration of the distinguishing truths of the gospel, is the most effectual means for the restoration of such characters to social comfort and usefulness, as well as to the hope of future felicity.

* Such improvidence is far from being confined to the wandering classes of the poor. It is greatly to be regretted, that those who have a fixed residence, have not more encouragement to form habits of frugality. It is seldom that they *could* lay by a little money; but when they have it, they know not how to secure it for a season of necessity, and therefore usually spend it extravagantly. If, in each market town, some benevolent person, of good property and established character, would take the trouble of receiving trifling sums on loan

PART III.

From her marriage, to her conversion.

———

I do not remember that any thing material happened for some time after this, till some of the travellers raised a false report concerning me, of which, the Lord knows, I was entirely innocent; and if he had not preserved me, I must have lost my life. I have reason to apprehend, that my husband got drunk on purpose to abuse me. We had a mile and a half to go to our lodging; and, although I was pregnant, he beat me all the way; and at last he kicked me down, and tried to choke me. Oh what a mercy that my life was spared, that I did not die under his hands, and he by the laws of his country—to have met and dwelt together in that awful place where hope never comes! My soul, wonder and adore! May the wonders of that love ever be the burden of my song, that snatched us both from imminent destruction; and, unworthy as I am, still gives me a humble hope, that, through what our great High Priest has done, we shall one day meet in glory, and dwell for ever there!*

from the neighbouring poor, to be repaid, whenever wanted, with interest; it would probably tend more than any other means, to induce them to lay by what they could occasionally spare.

* If the feelings which evidently prompted these reflections, be seriously compared with those, which a person naturally so stubborn

Soon after this I was delivered at Bradwin, near Towcester, of twins. A lady who lived there, was very kind to me; and gave me good advice and books. I felt some faint desires to profit by what I read; but when I returned to my husband and his wicked companions, my convictions died away; and I relapsed into my old courses, laid my books aside, and was so taken up with my two children, that I forgot my soul. My husband was very fond of them, and very kind to me, while they both lived, which was not long. In this lying-in, I lost my hearing;* and about three weeks after, one of my dear babies died in the bed with me: from what cause I cannot tell. This was a very severe affliction to me. I was almost distracted; but my heart was still insensible to the voice of Providence. I could weep and mourn for the loss of my child, but not for my sins.

: My husband pursued his former practices of drinking and swearing, till he impaired his health, and to all appearance was far gone in a decline. This obliged us to seek for help; and we applied to a famous doctor at Dallington, near Northampton, who told us he thought he could help him,

---

and haughty as the writer of this narrative, doubtless cherished, at the time of being treated with such brutality, they may afford a striking view of the change which a genuine knowledge of the gospel is capable of producing on the human mind, in its disposition toward fellow-creatures, as well as toward God.

  * From this infirmity she never was relieved, being always afterwards unable to converse without the use of an ear-trumpet.

if he was near enough to prescribe for him.* We were not able to get lodgings; and having a family of small children, and another family who travelled with us for company, whom we were loath to part with, as my husband's health was so bad, we scarcely knew what to do : but at length we agreed to build huts in the fields between Dal-lington and Wollaston, and there make our abode till his health might be restored. Our custom was, to go round the neighbouring villages, to sell our goods, and return at night. As the man who was with us made baskets, he used to stay at the tents. I had two small children, that could not follow me; so I left the elder under his care, and carried the younger in my arms : but oh, shocking to relate! whilst my husband, myself, and four children, were gone out, the poor man went from the huts, to seek the asses which carried our baggage; and left my dear baby by a little fire. When he returned, the huts were in flames, and he could not find her. He ran about, like a mad man, to seek her, but in vain; till, in his fright,

---

* Such people are not thinly scattered over the country. They usually pretend, on inspecting the urine of a sick person, immediately to ascertain the nature of the disease, and infallibly to cure it. A few instances of success, amidst whatever number of failures, commonly suffice to establish their reputation : and the poor often sacrifice the daily bread of their families to their reliance on the assurances of relief which are lavishly afforded by quacks of this description. The man who is here alluded to, was infamous for blasphemy; and either imagined, or wished others to believe, that he dealt with the devil.

D

he threw himself into the midst of the fire, and pulled her out alive. He said, " My dear baby! what must I do?" She, poor lamb! who was not three years old, made answer, "Carry me to my mother:" and he, almost senseless, threw her on his back, leaving the clothes and huts to burn; and ran, as fast as he could, to Wellingborough, whither he knew that we designed to go. He had much difficulty to find me; and when he did, he cried out, "Mary, your child's burnt to death!"* Oh my God! it was thou, and only thou, that sustained my senses through this awful scene. As my dear child was not quite dead, they provided us a lodging in the town. I believe every means was made use of to preserve her; but in a few days she died: and we lost, not only our child, but nearly every thing. We had not a garment left, to shift either ourselves or children; although before, we had some very good ones. A watch, and a large pair of silver buckles, which we had about us, was all that remained: and how gladly should we have given these to have restored the child! She was the survivor of our beloved twins; and twined round our hearts, like the ivy round the oak. If the Lord had not

* The editor has heard her say, that she was in a shop buying some small articles which they wanted, when the man with her child ran along the street, followed by a crowd of people, whom his outcries and strange appearance had drawn after him. Both the man and child were so disfigured by the effects of the fire, that she saw them without conjecturing who they were.

supported me, even when I neither loved nor feared him, it must have cost me my life; for I had a disorder in my head, that made me almost distracted. Blessed be the Lord! I trust it was a happy rod; a sanctified trial, that brought me to close and serious reflection: and though we were obliged to go into the hay country that summer, to earn ourselves and children some clothing, I determined afterwards to settle; and thought I would be very good.*

In the close of the summer, we came to Stony-Stratford; and after some trouble to obtain a settlement, we hired part of a house. Our beginnings were very small, as we had little to furnish it with: however, I was resolved to have a home for my children; and, through mercy, I was enabled to fulfill this purpose. My vows and promises, nevertheless, were soon forgotten, when my trouble wore off: only I used to pray, that if I bred again, I might have twins. To my shame, and with trembling I ought to write it, I returned to my former evil practices, as the dog to his vomit. To obscene jests, filthy ribaldry, and profane swearing, I was grossly addicted. Yet, so great were the patience and forbearance of a dear and compassionate Saviour to such a daring rebel, that he still strove with me; for though I had hardened myself against convictions, he sent

---

* By the hay country, is meant the vicinity of London, where the grass is earliest mown.

me first one monitor, and then another. I well remember, that I was either swearing, or making my jests, when my husband's sister, (not the same that I mentioned before, but another, who was herself a very wicked woman,) reproved me sharply; and told me, I might be ashamed of my conduct. This reproof exasperated me, as I (poor wretch!) thought myself far superior to her: yet it proved a word in season; for, through the goodness of God, it renewed my former convictions, and again led me to serious thought, and strong desires to alter my mode of life. I left off swearing, and began (in my way) to keep the sabbath, reading, and teaching my children. I thought this was all my duty; and as this change was almost instantaneous, I was soon observed by my neighbours, and was very proud of their praise. Thus I went on for some time, seeking acceptance by what I then thought my good works; knowing nothing of the holiness and spirituality of the law of God, the exceeding sinfulness of my best duties, or the way of a sinner's acceptance through Jesus Christ. I had never heard the gospel since I was a child; nor was I now at all desirous of it, as I thought my deafness a sufficient excuse for my absence from public worship; and that I was very good without it.

The next harvest, my husband went to his work; and as I was a pretty good reaper, he engaged some land, for me to reap, by the acre. I took my eldest child to make bands; she by some means highly displeased me, and provoked me to swear a dreadful oath; but ah! no sooner had I uttered it, than my spirits sunk within me, and I was stung with guilt. Having no one to whom I could tell my mind, my burden was intolerable; and, to complete my misery, soon after this, I fell into bad company, and drank too freely. When I began to reflect on my conduct, oh, how was I surrounded with terrors, and the awful flashes of a guilty conscience! What a compassionate Saviour have we to deal with! What a mercy it was, that he did not, at this time, bring the sins of my youth, with all their aggravated circumstances, into remembrance; and suffer me to sink in black despair! But, blessed be his name! he well knew what I had to contend with in my family-connexions; and therefore was pleased to lay no more on me than I was able to bear.*

How I went on, for some time after this, I have almost forgot; till one day, walking in the

---

* From this time, her moral reformation seems to have been decisive and uniform; although her knowledge of the gospel was evidently very imperfect, and her attention to religious truth was not yet such as tended to increase it. The change of her conduct appears to have been produced merely by conviction of the evil and danger of gross sin, and that only in reference to her late relapses, without a due abhorrence of the wickedness of her past life. So partial an effect on her conscience was not likely to have produced a permanent alteration of her course of life, if she had not soon been excited to use means of religious instruction.

fields with a female neighbour, one of my daughters who was with us, did something to displease me; and I asked her, what she thought would become of her, if she went on so? The woman turned short round to me, and said sharply, "And what do you think will become of *you?* You have more knowledge than your child; and ought to be found in your duty." I asked her, what she meant; she told me, I never attended at any place of worship. I answered, I had been at church to try, and could not hear. She said, that there was a meeting-house in the town, and I might stand on the pulpit-stairs; where she knew, I might hear. As soon as she mentioned the meeting-house, I thought I would go, and make a trial: accordingly I went the next sabbath; and finding that I could hear, I continued to attend. I soon began to be much persecuted, both by my husband, and our neighbours; but I did not care for that: for I wanted to flee from the wrath to come; though, as yet, I knew not the way. I do not remember that what I heard at the meeting-house was made of any use to me: but still I kept waiting, in much darkness and distress; crying to the Lord, in a poor broken way, for mercy.*   Blessed be his name! he heard my

---

* This, probably, is the best proof which could have been afforded, that either the doctrine which she heard, or else the mere attendance with seriousness on public worship, was of important use to her. The essential truths of the gospel always were preached at the Meeting-house where she then attended, and a suitable practice was likewise

groans, and directed me to a book, which, I trust, shewed me what I was, what I wanted, and where it was to be found. The title was, " An Alarm to Unconverted Sinners." I had never heard of this book ; but going into a neighbour's house, I saw it lie on the table, and took it up to read it : I had not power to put it down again, for it so exactly described my case, that, before I had read many lines, I was bathed in tears. I begged the owner to lend it me, which she readily did. I took it home, and found I had got a treasure of more solid worth than the mines of both the Indies. Here were the author's kind expostulation with the unconverted sinner ; his prayer for such ; the marks of the unconverted ; their miseries ; with means and motives to conversion ; shewing what *is* conversion, and what is *not* ; and closing with kind advice for family and personal godliness, and other excellent remarks and prayers.*

This book, the Lord was pleased to make of singular use to my soul ; for many a time have I

---

inculcated : but it appears, on the one hand, that the preacher did not adapt his style sufficiently to the understandings of his more ignorant hearers ; and, on the other, that the writer seems to have confounded the idea of spiritual usefulness, with that of sensible relief and comfort, which she might not yet be prepared to receive.

* This work of Mr. Alleine, a young minister in the seventeenth century, has often been reprinted. Its title, which tends to impede its general usefulness, might properly be exchanged for that of " A serious address on the subject of Conversion."

laid it before me, and wept, and prayed in bitterness of soul, because I feared that I was unconverted. Oh, how did I long, yea, pant and breathe to be converted! Sometimes, a gleam of hope broke in; at other times, gloomy fears prevailed. If I remember right, the first scriptural promise that afforded me encouragement to hope for salvation, was this;* " Because I live, ye shall live also." Sweet was that word "*shall*," to my soul! I derived strength from it, to persevere against great opposition and temptation. My poor husband was so much exasperated, because I would go to the Meeting-house, that when I came home, he has threatened to throw the boiling pot over me; and more than once, he took it off the fire for that purpose, but was always prevented. Oh, the goodness and mercy of God to such an unworthy creature, that has so often preserved me in imminent danger!

Though, in despite of persecution, I still went to meeting, I could not well understand the minister; his language being too much polished for my weak comprehension. At length, Mr. Wesley's preachers came to the town; and as their discourses were levelled to my capacity, there I fixed.† Although in general, my hopes were

---

* John xiv. 19.

† Let every preacher, whether of the Established Church, or a Dissenter, seriously revolve this part of the narrative. That the Methodists, during the last half century, both of Mr. Wesley's and Mr. Whitfield's parties, have been more successful in the reformation

low, yet I enjoyed some few very comfortable seasons under their ministry. And oh, how glad was I, when out on a journey, from under the eye of my poor husband, that I might attend on the word without distraction or opposition! I esteemed it more than my necessary food, and would at any time have gone without that, rather than miss an opportunity of hearing the word. For some time, however, I was greatly discouraged by severe domestic trials, which I *then* thought would not have been suffered to befal me, if I was a child of God :*. and though I did not give up all hope, nor was suffered to go back into the world again, I had many severe conflicts with temptations and fears. But, blessed be the Lord! he bore me up under all, and in his own due time manifested himself to be a God hearing and answering the prayers and feeble groans of a poor worm.

---

of the poor, than preachers of any other denomination,—it is apprehended, cannot be denied : while their distinguishing tenets differ more from each other, than either party is conceived to differ from the Church of England, or from a great majority of the Dissenters. Can the success which they have had in common, be rationally imputed to other means than the simplicity of their address, and the energy of their zeal ?

* How inconsistent is such an inference from temporal afflictions, with the tenor of the holy scriptures! Its frequency demonstrates only the strength of impressions that are made by present and sensible objects, compared with those which are derived from what is invisible and future.

I mentioned before, having prayed that I might have twins again; and now the Lord was pleased to grant my request. I was delivered of two girls, according to my wish: but though the Lord gave me my desire, he gave me occasion to learn, that it was not right to dictate to him; for through a hard labour, and bad nursing, it nearly cost me my life. In the beginning of my affliction, I was in deep distress of body and mind. My poor husband was at the alehouse most of his time; whilst I, and my children, wanted the common necessaries of life: but here the Lord interposed. A son, grown up, who had not been heard of for twelve months, (having eloped from a house in London where he had been bound apprentice) came home just at this time; and in some measure supplied his father's place, being very kind to me and the children. I was, at the same time, in great anguish of soul; fearing that I should die, and be finally lost. So great were my terrors, that I could not bear to be left alone one minute, if I could help it; and if I was, oh how did I pray, and cry, and wring my hands, and beseech the Lord to have mercy on me, and save my soul! I cannot better describe my feelings at this time, than as a weight, like a stone, at my heart; which I could by no means get rid of, till the Lord was pleased to relieve me from it.

Whilst I lay in this distressed situation, the Methodist preachers came to the town; and I sent for one, who very kindly attended me. I told him all my fears; and, after he had heard my experience, he very affectionately pointed me to the Lamb of God, that taketh away the sin of the world. He then went to prayer; and the Lord was pleased to give him such a spirit of supplication, that there was not a dry eye in the room,—though several very wicked people were present. But I am now come to the most pleasing part of my story; may the Lord help me to relate it with a single eye to his glory! That ever such a daring rebel should be so highly favoured, must be entirely ascribed to grace, free unmerited grace, and bleeding, dying love: for guilty, filthy, and unworthy as I am, I enjoyed such a delightful state of mind, soon after the minister had left the room, that I find myself at a loss to describe it. This I can well remember, that the weight I before complained of, was instantaneously removed; and my whole soul filled with peace and love: and at the same time, I had such a glorious view of the Saviour of sinners, as bleeding and dying on the cross, and of my interest in him; that my ravished spirit was filled with unutterable joy. I could not forbear telling all that were about me, or came to see me, what God had done for my soul. But this seemed only to stir up enemies from every quarter; yea even those who, I have good ground to hope, truly feared God, not feeling the same joys, were ready to silence me; for not only my neighbours, but my own family reported, that I was actually mad.

Though I, on account of my deafness, could not hear them, my friends could; and this grieved them so, that they were at a loss how to act. I begged hard that they would send for the minister, that I might tell him my joys; but they were so intimidated, that they dared not send for him. They could not, however, take away my Saviour's presence. My poor body was brought extremely low, so that none expected my life, from one day to another. Yet now I wished to be alone, as much as before I feared it; that I might enjoy my comforts, and prepare for eternity. And oh, how did I long to depart, and to be with Christ! My dear boy, whom I tenderly loved, and some of my other children, came weeping round me; and though I could not help dropping a sympathetic tear over those that were so dear to me, yet so great was my desire to be gone, that I could freely and gladly have left them in the kind hand of providence.

An event then occurred, which I think it not proper to omit; though I cannot tell how to account for it, nor do I expect that I ever shall in this world. I was so near death, that I was stretched out, and to all appearance dying apace. I was crying, " Come Lord Jesus, come quickly!" when I again fell into a kind of swoon, and thought I heard these words distinctly: " To-morrow thou shalt be with me in paradise." When I was a little revived, I told my friends, that I should not survive Friday, and ardently longed for the happy moment. But the Lord's thoughts were above my thoughts; and he, for wise ends, best known to himself, was pleased to detain me a little longer. Oh that it may be to his praise and glory! But as I did not expire when I expected that I should, the enemy had now got a handle indeed, and stirred up one of my children, with my husband, to raise false reports. As the great doctor was then in the town,* he came to see me, and pronounced me quite distracted; he ordered all my books to be taken away; which my daughter told him were fifteen, though I had but two, which were taken from me. The Lord, nevertheless, supported me: and though I was sorely afflicted, and persecuted, my inward consolations were great, and bore me up under all.

Soon after this, one of my twins died; and the other was so near death, that I more than once thought her gone: but she and I were raised up, to the surprise of every body. I was long confined before I could come down stairs again, among my family. My poor husband was all this time usually drinking and swearing at an ale-house; and when he did come to me, which was but seldom, it was only to upbraid and threaten to throw me out of the window, if I did not get up and do for my family. I was not so much grieved for myself as for him; his spiritual condition now lying very near to my heart. To satisfy

* An eminent surgeon now living in Northamptonshire.

him, I came down stairs, before I was fit to do so; and the first thing that attracted my attention, was a book, which, by mistake, had been left on the table. I eagerly seized it, and thought I had got a treasure; and though I was fearful of being detected, I ventured to open it. It was a Hymn-book; and the hymn I opened at was exactly suited to my case.* It is impossible to describe my sensations while reading it. It was as a cordial to my soul, and the means, under God, of prompting me to press on, through all my trials and difficulties; which, the Lord knows, were not few. But, blessed be the name of the Lord! my comforts were proportionable; and he helped me to go on my way rejoicing, through evil or good report. The word, the ordinances, and the people of God, were the joy of my soul. In this sweet frame of spirit I continued many months.†

---

* Mr. Wesley's Collection, hymn 29. "Where shall my wondering soul begin?" &c.

† Without pretending to ascertain the precise time of her conversion from sin and ignorance to the knowledge and love of God, the Editor has here introduced a pause in the Narrative, at a period when that important change appears to have been effectually accomplished. The reader may judge of the congruity of this event with the expressions of the sacred scriptures, and decide for himself whether it does not tend to illustrate those which speak of being born again, created anew in Christ Jesus, passed from darkness to marvellous light, and from death to life. Let him reflect that the new testament represents such a change as essential to real christianity : " If any man be in Christ, he is a new creature : old things are passed away ; behold, all things are become new :" and that our Lord himself has said, " Except a man be born again, he cannot see the kingdom of God."

PART IV.

From her conversion, to the death of her husband.

———

GLAD was I now, when I was able to travel again; that I might enjoy the company and

———

The real change of principle, affections, and conduct, which appears to be denoted by these expressions, and to be exemplified in this narrative, should, however, be carefully distinguished from the circumstances attending such a change, in the present, or in any other particular instance. It is the attainment of the end, not the means, or the manner of attaining it, that is of essential importance. Many individuals have been brought from a course of sin to genuine holiness, without those strong emotions, either of terror or of joy, which the subject of this narrative felt, and has described. Her astonishing transition from the greatest profligacy, and the natural force of her passions, doubtless concurred to produce those sensations. Instances, on the other hand, are happily not uncommon, in which persons have been so seriously impressed from early childhood with the truths of the gospel, as very gradually, and almost imperceptibly, to have become established christians.

In some degree, the Editor apprehends moreover, enthusiasm was mingled with genuine piety, in what has been related; and he is aware that feelings very similar to some of those here described, have been evinced by persons who afterwards relapsed into sin, and died without affording satisfactory proofs of repentance. The circumstances mentioned in p. 35. are particularly referred to, by this remark. In the writer's inference from a strong impression of a passage of scripture, she was evidently mistaken. But whatever portion of uncertainty, or even of delusion, may appear in such instances, they cannot reasonably be regarded as derogating from the solid piety which she exemplified throughout the remainder of her life. Without resembling her in this respect, it is in vain for any one to indulge a hope respecting eternity, or a prospect of permanent comfort in this world. It is evident, that religion was to the writer of this narrative, the source of consolation, peace, and joy, amidst complicated afflictions. As such, it is recommended to us in the scriptures; and such it is found to be at this day, by those who bring it to the test of personal experience, by committing their souls to God, in well-doing.

conversation of serious christians; and, praise to his name, the Lord gave me favour in the eyes and hearts of his people and ministers; and whilst they rejoiced with me at what God had done for my soul, I found their edifying conversation, and fervent prayers, truly profitable and precious. Many refreshing seasons I have enjoyed, with my bible in my hand, as I have walked from town to town: so that I could with propriety have adopted those sweet lines, which I have read in Dr. Watts's Lyric Poems:

"Here, I could say,
　　And point the ground whereon I stood,
Here, I receiv'd a visit half the day,
　　From my descending God."*

And oh, how have I longed to tell my fellow-sinners, "what a dear Saviour I had found!"

My poor husband now was constantly in my mind; and so ardently did I desire the salvation of his soul, that I could scarcely refrain from falling on my knees, to pray for him, as I walked on the road. Many precious texts occurred to my recollection, which encouraged me to go on praying; and one in particular, that I well remember has often refreshed my spirits. Joel iii. 21. "For I will cleanse their blood, that I have not cleansed; for the Lord dwelleth in Zion." Oh, how did I long and pray, that the Lord would accomplish this good word toward my husband! I have

---

* Watts's Horæ Lyricæ. Book i. Hope in darkness.

thought, when on a journey, that I should see an alteration in his conduct when I returned; but ah! instead of seeing my wishes fulfilled, perhaps I have found him in a worse disposition than when I left him. As soon as we met, he would begin swearing at me, for something the poor children had done in my absence; which I could not help, yet was to be blamed, and to suffer for. The enemy of souls also seemed to suggest to me,—"You see your prayers and tears are all lost; the man is worse and worse." But, blessed be the Lord! he was pleased to support me, and help me still to persevere, praying, and hoping against hope; till he saw it good to visit us with an alarming providence, which deeply affected both my husband and me.

My dear boy, whom I mentioned before, as having been so kind to me, was, one Sabbath morning, in all the bloom of youth, in health and spirits; and on Tuesday evening, a lifeless corpse. The circumstances that attended his death, were worthy of notice: but for brevity's sake, I omit them; in order to relate something respecting his father. Suffice it to say, to the praise and glory of a prayer-hearing and answering God, though the time of his illness was so short, there was hope in his end; and I humbly trust that I shall meet him in glory.

This death deeply affected his poor father, as the child, with his dying breath, begged him not to swear; and added, " Mother, pray." If I remember right, my husband left off swearing for a season. I know that he asked me to pray for him; and joined with me in family-prayer for some time: till at length his convictions wore off, with his trouble, which was very transient; and he returned to his former courses, which soon impaired his health. We made use of every means in our power for his relief, but all proved ineffectual, and he was soon far gone in a deep decline. I was now sent to the doctor at Dallington, as the last resource; and though I had little to bear my expenses, the Lord took care for me. I well remember going by a fine spring; I was very faint and weary, and I thought, cannot the Lord refresh my body by a draught of this water? I then took a crust, and asking his blessing, kneeled down, and took a hearty draught. I returned thanks; and praise to his name! found myself so much refreshed, that I went on the rest of my journey with great pleasure; and what was best of all, I trust I can say, I had much of his sacred presence, who is fairer than the sons of men. Oh, how did I long to tell to all the world what I then felt and experienced !

When I came back to Northampton, as I slept with a woman who had made a religious profession many years, I ventured to tell her some of my feelings: but I found her an entire stranger to my language, and she sorely grieved me. I expected, as she was an old professor, that she would rejoice in what God had done for my soul: but, instead of this, she seemed to doubt the truth of what I told her; and said, that she did not live on frames or feelings; she lived on Christ.*   But to my pain and grief, young as I was in experience, I could plainly perceive, that, however she might profess to live on Christ, she was not very careful to glorify him in her life and conversation.   This both distressed and staggered me; but, bless the Lord! he helped me to go on rejoicing, notwith-standing the combined efforts of earth and hell to retard my progress.

I now returned to Stony Stratford, with the medicines for my poor husband; but they were of no benefit.   He still grew worse and worse; yet he would not believe it, but always thought he should be better.   The doctor ordered him to take air and exercise; and he did so, till he could not walk many steps without crutches.   Yet he still persisted in swearing, with death almost in his countenance.   One day in particular, I think it was about six weeks before he died, he was cursing me in a most dreadful manner; and I trembled on his account.   My spirit was stirred

---

* It is not improbable that some degree of enthusiasm might be in-troduced into the writer's communications at that season: but a pious and reflecting mind would not on that account have discredited or disparaged the substance of them.   The phrase of "not living on frames and feelings," is but too often a canting excuse for insensi-bility, indifference, and indolence, in religion.   Genuine faith in Christ realises the objects of hope, as well as establishes the convic-tion of invisible things.   Hebrews xi. 1.

within me : I went up to him ; and with a mixture
of grief and indignation told him, I dared not
deceive him, for I could plainly see he was dying
apace : all the means used for his recovery proved
ineffectual ; and what could he think would become of his immortal soul ? If he died in that
state, where could he think to go to? He said,
to heaven, he hoped, as God was very merciful.
I endeavoured, as well as I could, to convince
him, that his hope was vain, false, and delusive ;
that God was just, as well as merciful ; and had
expressly said, that nothing unholy or unclean
should ever enter the heavenly state. I appealed
to his conscience, whether he then loved the
people of God, their company and conversation ?
He could not say that he did. " Then, (said I) how
do you think you should love to be in heaven,
where there is nothing but holiness to the Lord ;
no drunken, revelling companions there ; but all
is as one continued act of adoring love and praise."
I also informed him, that I durst by no means deceive him in regard to his recovery ; for his disorder, which was a decline, made such rapid progress, that it baffled the art of the most able phy-
sicians, so that there remained no hope.* I begged
him, therefore, if he had any love for his own
soul, to cry earnestly to the Lord to have mercy
on him, and grant him true repentance, and faith

---

* The gentleman mentioned p. 37, had prescribed for him, during
this illness.

in the Lord Jesus Christ, before it was too late ;
for consistently with his word he cannot save a
sinner in any other way : and much more to the
same purpose, which I cannot now so well remember." Glory be to God ! it had the desired effect.
Soon after I had left speaking, and had turned
from him, I happened to look round, and saw
that he had gone out. I asked my surviving boy,
who was present, where his father was ; he said that
he was gone up-stairs. I gently followed him to
the stair-head ; when, to my unspeakable comfort, I saw him on his knees, apparently wrestling
in prayer, which I had no room to doubt from
his conduct afterwards. When he came down-
stairs, he began talking with me very seriously,
and seemed to be much affected ; saying, that he
hoped he should no longer neglect his precious
soul, but would, if spared, go and see our
minister, who at that time was Mr. T—. My
joy was so great, on hearing this, that it almost
overcame me ; and I spoke unadvisedly, expres-
sing my doubt that the enemy would not suffer it.
But the Lord, who had begun the work, was
pleased to rebuke my unbelieving fears, by giving
him courage to fulfill his promise, and by suffer-
ing me to sink into such a dastardly, cowardly
frame, that I was really ashamed to go with him,
because we had to pass by a black-smith's shop,
where he used to associate with wicked companions. I thought that they would make sport
at us, and say I had turned him at last : so I made

an excuse to turn back for something, and to my
shame went creeping after him.

When we came to Mr. T.'s, he was absent
from home : but there was a serious young man,
who very kindly gave my husband such advice
and instructions as suited his case; and wrote
down several portions of scripture, for me to read
to him. He then prayed with him; and my husband joined very heartily. Oh, how it rejoiced
my soul, to see him, that a little before, had not
only been an enemy, but a bitter persecutor, ex-
press such cordial respect, and shake hands so
heartily with the young man at parting! Surely
none but he who made the heart, could produce
so sudden a change.

This was the Lord's doing, and it was marvellous in the eyes of many; particularly of his old
companions : for though they gazed and wonder-
ed, and I doubt not hated the change, yet the
Lord stopped their mouths, that they could say
nothing against it, at least nothing that came to
my knowledge. From this time, he was almost
continually engaged in prayer; this seemed to
be his most delightful exercise; and he became
so fond of my poor company, that he could hardly
bear my absence, even when the affairs of my
family called me away. One time, in particular,
as I sat near him, I saw his lips move; and knowing him to be very ignorant, I thought he said
some prayer that he had learned by rote. I said,
" My dear, what do you pray for; are you saying

the Lord's prayer?" Not that I slighted the Lord's prayer; I love and revere it: but I wanted to know whether he was merely praying by rote, or had a feeling sense of his misery, and the need he had of a Saviour. He replied, "No, I was not saying the Lord's prayer; I pray to be washed in the precious blood of Christ, and to be cleansed from this load of sin." I cannot now tell what answer I made him; but judge ye that know the love of Christ, what pleasing sensations I then felt! To see the dear man whom I loved next to my own soul, and over whom I had been for years weeping and groaning: to see him, I say, thus humble, and seeking salvation through the blood of the Lamb; oh it filled my whole soul with wonder, love and praise! At last, I broke out, and said, "Oh, my dear, this is a precious prayer; and if it comes from the heart, it will surely be answered in the Lord's time." And, blessed be the Lord! he went on still praying and hoping. His very aspect was altered! He used to be of a fierce, lion-like countenance: but now he was gentle as a lamb; and I do not remember that he ever once com_plained of his afflictions after this, though they were very severe. Yea, so tender was his conscience, that he would not take a little good beer, to comfort him, when he exceedingly wanted it; always saying, it had been his ruin, and therefore he would not touch it. Neither could he bear the company or conversation of his old associates; it always seemed disgusting to him: and he would gently chide me, if I conversed freely with them, when they came to see him. One woman, that used to be an old pot-companion, offered to assist in laying him out: but he begged earnestly that she might not be suffered to touch him when he was dead; and would not be satisfied till I promised that she should not. By keeping my word, I incurred much abuse.

My poor dear husband now became gradually worse. I was much cast down, and said to him, "Oh my dear, if it were the Lord's will to spare you, how happy should I be in such a dear partner!" He said, "Mary! don't say so; perhaps if I should live, I should be as wicked as ever; don't pray for my life; I had rather die, and go to Jesus." Soon after this, he took to his bed; and never came down more, till he was brought down for his burial: but, blessed be God! he still retained his reasoning faculties, and was enabled to pour out his soul in prayer. Once, in particular, as I was busy in my family, he knocked, for me to come to him. I went to him, and too hastily said, "What do you want?" He feebly answered, "I want you to pray;" I said, "I hope I do pray;" and went to my family again: but he soon knocked again; and I, oh wretch that I was! ran to him, and with a degree of impatience, asked, "What do you want?" He replied, "I want you to pray; and you must pray, as I pray;" and immediately, as if he had gathered all his small remaining strength, he raised himself on

his elbow, and poured out his soul before God.
Although I had not heard him, without a trumpet,
for some time, yet now the Lord helped him to ex-
alt his voice, so that I heard with ease: and I had
great reason to praise the Lord that I did hear
him. Oh, how sweetly did the Spirit assist him
to plead for the pardon of his numerous sins,
through the Saviour's blood; and to bemoan his
own vileness! Thus he prayed, till he was quite
exhausted. He then lay down; and said, " Now
do *you* pray." Nor would he suffer me to leave
the room, till I had spent some time in prayer
with him.

From that day, he was so very weak, that he
could not speak to be understood; and I could
learn but little of the state of his mind: but by
his looks, which were very expressive and mourn-
ful, I thought the tempter was busy, trying to mar
his hopes, and rob his soul of comfort. About
the same time, he lost the use of one of his arms.
In this state he remained, I think, the last time
that Mr. T—t visited him. When asked how he
was, he would shake his head, and seem much
distressed. Blessed be the Lord, he laid him on
his dear people's hearts, and encouraged such a
worm as me to wrestle for him; and at last was
pleased to answer our requests, to my exceeding
joy.

On Saturday morning, we began to perceive his
near approach to death. I was very anxious to
know how he was in his mind, and asked him:

F

but he could not speak, so as to be understood; and the persons who were with us thought that I disturbed him, and therefore wished me to leave the room. I accordingly went down, and did not see him till two o'clock in the afternoon. A neighbour then came down-stairs, and I enquired if he was dead? She answered, "No; and by his looks, I think he wants to see somebody." I said, "If he wants to see me, none shall keep me from him;" and I ran up-stairs directly. He soon perceived me; and, to my great surprise, put out his lame hand, to beckon me. I went up close to him; and finding that his reason was not impaired, I asked him how his mind was affected, in the near views of death and eternity? I said, "My dear love, is Christ precious and present in the dark valley? Are you happy in his love?" He could not speak, but put out his hand. I sat by him, and wept; but this he would not suffer: and I verily believe that he was then rejoicing; for, though he could not speak, he again put out his hand, and looked on me; as if he would have said, "Weep not for me; but rather rejoice, that I shall soon quit this vile clog of sin; and my ransomed spirit shall join in the praises of my exalted Redeemer." I had frequently asked him to give me some token, if he found the Lord present, when he was near his end: and at length I thought I knew his meaning. I said, "My dear, what is your meaning by thus putting out your hand? Do you want to make us understand how happy you are in the dark valley, and how near and dear Jesus is in this last conflict? If this be your intention, lift up your hand again, that all about us may see and know that religion is not a fable, but a true and substantial reality, that can support even in death." He instantly threw up his hand as high as he could reach. My heart was full; I could stay no longer; but was constrained to retire, and give vent to my feelings. As I withdrew, I said, " Oh! what a God do I serve," and well I might; for though this was a bereaving providence, yet it was truly a profitable season to my soul; and I trust we shall both join to praise the Lord for it, to all eternity.*

This was the parting struggle, and I never more saw him alive. He was seized with convulsions a few moments after I left the room, and soon expired. Thus was I left, a poor disconsolate widow, with five children, four of them young; and though I had much cause to rejoice, respecting my dear husband, yet I had many and sharp trials; and suffered much persecution. But, blessed be

---

* In very few instances, probably, are the evidences of repentance on a death-bed, so clear and satisfactory, as in this case. Like that of the penitent thief at the cross, it can afford no excuse for presumption or negligence, while young or in health : but it exhibits a hope of mercy to those who, at the approach of death, implore deliverance from sin ; and encouragement to those who constantly pray for their thoughtless relatives, to persevere, even to the last, in pleading with God on their behalf. John Saxby died about Michaelmas, 1782.

the Lord! he was my rock and refuge, yea my strong tower of defence: so that I was not at all terrified by my adversaries.

But I had other things to grapple with: I was left deeply in debt, with a small family to provide for; and was persuaded by some, that I had no right to pay what my husband had owed, as I was circumstanced: but the Lord, I trust, was my guide. I sold what I had, and discharged all our debts; except a few shillings at alehouses, that I knew nothing of till afterwards. I then applied to the parish for assistance: and, for a short time, they gave me three shillings weekly, but soon reduced this allowance.

PART V.

From the death of her husband, to that of her son.

HAVING obtained credit for some fresh goods, I proposed to travel with them toward London, to see my relations; who had been exceedingly kind to me, on our first settling at Stratford: but though I was permitted to set out on my intended journey, the Lord had ordered it otherwise. When I had walked a few miles, I saw a crowd of people on the rise of a hill before me, which alarmed me: and when I came up to them, my terror increased; for a poor travelling woman had died suddenly on the road, and they required my help to lift her into a cart. This, together with my own trouble, so affected me, that I know not how I got to Bow-brickhill, which was the place I meant first to stop at, on the way to London. All that day, after seeing the corpse, these words remained in my thoughts, " But thy life will I give unto thee for a prey, in all places whither thou goest :"* and when I entered Bow-brickhill, they impressed my mind so strongly, that I could not but apprehend something extraordinary would happen. As soon as I got to my friend's house, I was taken very ill ; and was detained three weeks, where I thought of staying but one night. I probably should not so particularly have remembered this circumstance, had it not been for what followed. Here I was visited by friends, whose kind attentions in part mitigated the grief and care that I felt for my poor children, whom I had left behind at Stony Stratford ; and helped me to bear my affliction with composure, though at the first it was very heavy. Here I first became acquainted with my kind friend Mr. C—y of Woburn ; to

* Jer. xlv. 5.—The writer, like many persons of real piety, but of little knowledge and strong imagination, was evidently prone to regard texts of scripture that occurred forcibly to her recollection as predictive of her own future circumstances. In one instance, she had already found her application of such passages groundless, and hurtful ; some of them are expunged from her narrative ; and the present is designed, not as a pattern for imitation, but as an indication of the actual state of her mind.

whose medical assistance, under God, I think I have reason to ascribe my being restored to health, much sooner than I should otherwise have been. May the Lord bless and reward him, and his, for all their love to, and care over, such a worm as I!

When I was able to get up, I longed to be with my poor dear children, who were near my heart; and as I had a kind and dear friend at Newport-Pagnel, to call on, I, with the Lord's help, got so far the first day; but was forced to stop the next, to gather strength. Through the goodness of God, and my friend's kindness, I then got home to my family; but was immediately taken ill again, and was not able to work for fourteen weeks. I had four children to provide for; and cannot remember that I had any thing more of the parish, than three shillings a week. But, bless the Lord! he raised me up good friends: and as soon as I was able to crawl about, one and another would give me a shilling; and even my poor husband's old companions, seeing me look so ill, would pay me something they had owed us in his life-time. Thus goodness and mercy have followed poor unworthy me! One instance in particular, which, whenever I think of it awakens my gratitude, I think I ought not to omit. While I was getting better, though very slowly, the Rev. Mr. T—t was ordained. The service was long; and I had nothing, that I could eat, in the house; so I could not take any refreshment with me: and when I was coming away, very faint, and saw abundant provisions that had been prepared for the friends who came from considerable distances, I thought—Oh, that some of them would be so kind as to send me a morsel, to recruit my weary body! All, however, seemed to be too much engaged to think on me. But the Lord inclined the heart of one that was by no means a friend to religion, to send me a plate of nice food. I asked the child that received it, who sent it? And when she informed me, I had scarcely power to eat it, amidst tears of gratitude to my heavenly Benefactor, for his bounty to such a worm as me, just at the moment that I so greatly needed it.

After this, the Lord was pleased to raise up friends that were very kind to me, and mine; particularly Mr. and Mrs. T—t. My poor children proved very refractory; and Mrs. T—t was so good as to manage some of them, when I was on journeys. To others, they gave their schooling; which was a great help: and in every respect, their kindness was great. One of these valuable friends, I hear, is gone to receive her reward; and may the Lord pour every blessing on the head of the other, in rich abundance, both in time and eternity! About the same time, if I remember right, my good friends the Methodists left Stratford, as they saw but little fruit of their labours; though I believe that there are yet a few who continue to this day. I now attended Mr. T.'s ministry constantly, except when I was on journeys; and was almost persuaded in my own mind to join the church under his care; as there were several added, and numbers attended. The Meeting-house also was enlarged; and all things seemed to prosper. But ah! there was soon cause to adopt those lines of the Rev. Mr. Newton;

" Once, whilst we aim'd at Zion's ways,
" A sudden mourning check'd our tongues."

Surely I can say, for one, it was as deep a wound to my soul, as ever I met with in all my life. I had been on a journey, and was coming home. A person on the road asked me, if I had heard that Mr. T. had lost most of his hearers. I answered "No; nor could I believe it." However, to my grief, I found it too true. Not being a church-member, nor having any thing to do on either side, I shall only speak of the sorrow which it caused me, to observe, that where harmony, love, and peace, had so lately made their happy abode, now there was nothing but disorder, confusion, strife, and debate. As I was young in experience, and knew little, either of the devices of Satan, or the plague of my own heart, it so staggered me, that I was often fearful I should at last give up all my profession. For I saw, and heard, things in the temper and conduct of professors, so much unlike the meek and lowly Jesus, that I have often cried and prayed to the Lord, to know if there could be a real christian among them or not. Whilst matters were thus going on, I used to travel into the country, as often as I could; it being almost too much for my feelings, to see the friends I so tenderly and dearly loved, in such grief and distress. Yet the Lord was pleased to support them under all. Mr. T. in particular, was carried above his troubles, in such a remarkable manner, that he appeared not only cheerful, but sometimes very happy: so true is the Lord to his sacred word of promise, "My grace is sufficient for thee;" and, "As thy days, so shall thy strength be." I now went on my way very heavily; being both grieved and stumbled: yet was witness to many gracious appearances of a kind providence, both for myself and friends. But, ah! so stubborn, so refractory and rebellious was I, that, like a bullock unaccustomed to the yoke, I was ready to kick, under every fresh trouble; and, to my shame, too often lost sight of my mercies. Oh, what a blessing it was, that the Lord did not say, "Let her alone, my spirit shall no more strive with so ungrateful a creature!" Oh, praise to his unlimited grace and unbounded goodness, that has still kept me, though feebly halting, in the good way, amidst so many briars and thorns, as I have been entangled with in this wilderness! Not unto me, not unto me, Lord, but to thy name be the glory and the praise!

I now used to go to Olney, and attend occasionally on the Rev. T. H—ll—d's ministry; and I found it so much blest to my soul, that I longed to live at Olney, in order to enjoy it constantly.

I could not bear the thought of leaving Stratford, whilst my friends were there; neither could I see my way clear to do so. But some time after this, Mr. T. had a call to a distant part of the country; and when I saw his goods on sale, I thought I would not be long at Stratford; but still was fearful lest I should take a wrong step. Whilst I was deliberating, a circumstance occurred, which I thought quite cleared my way. I lived in a house belonging to the officers of the parish: one of my children was married, and gone from me; my poor boy was at Olney, apprentice; and I had but two to provide for at home. The parish officers had long before taken off my weekly money, and now they wanted the house; and threatened, that, if I did not remove, they would put a man and his wife, and six children, into it with me. I thought, that I might as well pay rent at Olney, as at Stratford; and my poor boy was very importunate for my removal thither. There were two young women likewise, that were much attached to me, at Stratford; and when I happened to mention it to them, and my children, they would have no refusal; but insisted on going to Olney with me, to help me to pay my rent. So to Olney we came.* I thought I was doing the will of God; and prayed, and hoped, that my new house might be indeed a Bethel.

I now, by the assistance of kind friends, went into a little business; thinking to leave off tra-

* April 30, 1791.

velling, as I had been some years subject to a disorder which rendered it difficult: but I soon
found that my shop would not answer, so I was
obliged to go out when I was able. I met with
great trouble at home, from the contrariety of
tempers I had to deal with; and instead of my
house being a Bethel, according to my hopes and
desires, it soon became a Beth Aven. Still, in
my poor way, I kept up family prayer, and reading the word; but to my grief, it had not the
desired effect. Many a time have I crept, as it
were, to the throne of grace; and in bitter anguish
of soul poured out my prayers, to be kept from
resentment and anger: and perhaps, as soon as I
came into my family, directly fell into what I had
been so earnestly praying against. The young
persons who came with me, from whom I expected so much comfort, were both of them heavy
trials. One, in particular, I often entreated to
leave me; but she would not: and, what with
her, and my own children, my life became bur-
densome; my flesh wasted; and, what was worse,
I feared I should be suffered to bring a reproach
upon the gospel. As I had joined the church
under Mr. H——'s care, I expected every day
to be severely censured, or set aside; and even
dreaded the sight of the deacons, or my dear pastor. Oh, what a mercy it was, under the complicated trials I then met with, that I did not sink
into absolute despair; but was still supported,
and though faint, yet kept feebly pursuing! Not

unto me, Lord! not unto me, but to thy name be all the glory! I had many reasonings in my own mind, about coming to Olney; and thought I had taken a wrong step, and that the Lord was con-tending with me for so doing: and indeed, I have still reason to fear, that I came full of pride and self, looking to the minister, and the means, instead of the God of means; and the Lord, justly jealous for his own glory, hath been writing Marah on all my creature comforts. Yea those very means of grace, which I so fondly almost doated on, have often been occasions of grief to my soul; either by feeling no appetite for them, or by my wicked heart wandering whilst apparently engaged in them, and by coming away, as it were, all leanness and barrenness. May the good Lord forgive the iniquity of my most holy things!

About this time, if I remember right, I had a fall from a waggon; which confined me to my room for several weeks. Every one that came to see me, as well as the doctor that attended me, said they scarcely ever beheld such a miracle of mercy: for I fell on my forehead; and, as the ground was frozen, it was a matter of astonishment that I was not killed on the spot. But the Lord had something more for his poor worm to suffer; and therefore gave me strength to bear this affliction. The news was soon carried to my poor boy, who came almost in a state of distraction; and to see the tenderness and affection of that dear child, caused me almost to realise the parting struggle: for I did not think I should recover. All my poor children were much affected; but my dear boy was so greatly distressed, that I felt for him as much as for myself. When he had any spare time, he would be with me. I must not forget the Lord's goodness in this season of trial. Praise to his dear name! he not only supported, but for the most part gave me strong consolation; so that though my pains were very great, I was kept from murmuring, and had some sweet seasons of rejoicing, both alone, and with the dear friends, when they came to visit me. Although I was willing to live, if the Lord saw good, I almost dreaded going into the world again. The Lord was pleased, however, to raise me up; and when I got about, I found my business in such a state, that I must either leave it off, or be likely to break: so, as soon as I could make up matters, I sold off, and paid my creditors; except a small sum, which two of them were so obliging as to remit, because they said I dealt honestly; which the Lord gave me strength to do, and to his name be all the glory!

Before I had this fall, if I remember right, one of the young persons who came with me to Olney left us. I believe that she is a real christian; though from one trouble or another, we were suffered to hurt one another's mind. We have been cordial friends ever since we parted. Soon after, one of my daughters married; and the other

G

young person that lived with us, also married shortly afterwards. I removed, therefore, with my youngest child, into a smaller house ; and was now promising myself much comfort : as I was delivered from some very great burdens, and lived near my poor dear boy, in whom, I must own, I too much delighted. But ah! my domestic happiness was very transient; for scarcely were we well settled in our new habitation, when my poor girl, who set out to work, on Saturday, June 28, 1794, came home about noon, crying most sadly. I was exceedingly anxious to know the cause; but could get no answer, till a dear friend who came with her, ventured to tell me that my son had had a misfortune. It was a mercy to me, at that moment, that I could form no idea of her meaning; but thought my dear child had only got a slight hurt : but as soon as his sister had regained her speech, she told me plainly that he was drowned.*

---

* Thomas Saxby, the youth who was thus suddenly cut off, was then in the eighteenth year of his age, of unimpeachable moral conduct, and of the most amiable disposition. He was very fond of bathing, and peculiarly desirous of learning to swim : but his mother, being apprehensive that he might fall into danger, usually made him promise, at the commencement of each summer, that he would not bathe during that season; to which he invariably adhered. This precaution she omitted in 1794, and he therefore considered himself at liberty to gratify his inclination. His fellow-apprentice, who could swim well, accompanied him to the water, during their hour of dinner; and seeing him sink, (it is supposed from a seizure by the cramp) immediately dived after him; but could not raise him, and totally exhausted his own strength in the attempt. It is said, however, that he was not more than ten minutes under water. It appears, therefore, probable, that if the means appointed by the Royal

This did not, at first, seem to affect me, so much as might have been expected ; as I then thought he had only fallen into the water, and that they were gone to recover him. So kind was the Lord to unworthy me, that I did not feel all the weight of my trouble at once ; but it came on as it were gradually. Before they brought my poor child home, as soon as I could get a moment's liberty, I flew to my long-experienced refuge, the throne of grace ; and though it was with much confusion, poured out my soul to my gracious Lord, that he in mercy would strengthen me to bear the trial with patience and composure. Whilst I was in my closet, (Mr. U. of London, Mr. H. being from home) came to see and condole with me : and

---

Humane Society had been used, he might have been restored. As the proper method of proceeding in such cases is by no means generally known, and as it is possible that the lives of some fellow creatures may be preserved by inserting here a paper which has been circulated in this vicinity, no other apology is offered for annexing it.

Thomas constantly attended on public worship with his master, a wheelwright, at the Baptist meeting-house in Olney. His mother having joined the Independent congregation, and the youth being buried in the Church-yard, the Vicar, and the two Dissenting Ministers of the town, testified their regard both to the living and the dead, by preaching a funeral sermon on the occasion, at each place of worship, from the same text, 2 Kings iv. 26.

It seems proper here to observe, that Mary had become a dissenter, not from any dislike to the established church, but because her difficulty of hearing could be better accommodated in a dissenting place of worship. She always discovered the most cordial respect for pious ministers and people, of every class ; and was reciprocally esteemed by them, without any discrimination of parties. May the same spirit universally prevail, however decidedly each may prefer the body with which he is more closely connected !

though it is to my shame and disgrace, I will honestly record, that, because the minister found me on my knees, that monster pride sprung up, and I felt elated, even in those most trying moments. May the good Lord pardon the iniquity of my holy things, subdue my pride, and wash all my polluted services in his precious blood! And may he bless his dear servant, who was so kind as to visit, and pray with and for me, several times, though I was an entire stranger to him.

The news was now carried to my married daughter, who lived near us, and was pregnant at the time. She came, in order to learn the truth of the report; and, if I remember right, my dear boy was just then brought home on a hurdle. She was subject to fits; and immediately fell into them. Her sister was so affected, that I could not bear the house, but was forced to leave it. And oh, judge ye that know any thing of parental affection, what were my feelings at that dismal moment! I ran from house to house, like a distracted creature; and though all pitied, none could help, or ease my pain, but that God, who has said, "Call upon me in the day of trouble; I will deliver thee, and thou shalt glorify me." And oh, help me to praise his name! he was faithful to his promise. On sabbath morning, as I lay on my bed, weeping over my afflictions, the sun arose, and shone most brilliantly. Ah! thought I, there is nothing in the world of nature, that can afford me one moment's comfort; I will arise and go to the Lord, and see if I can find any comfort from him. I did so; and, for ever blessed be the compassionate Saviour! he heard my broken groans, and applied this precious cordial to my wounded soul; "My grace is sufficient for thee, my strength shall be made perfect in thy weakness." These words infused such a measure of fortitude into my helpless mind, that I rose from my knees, not only strengthened, but much comforted; and I was enabled to attend the morning prayer-meeting, and to hear Mr. U. three times that sabbath. When my other children who lived at Stratford came, it was again almost too much for my feelings; yet the Lord supported me.

We had another trying scene on Monday. As my poor boy's corpse could not be kept, the coroner came in the morning; and though it was the largest fair in the year, we were obliged to carry him through the midst of it, to his long home. No one knows what I felt, while such a concourse of people followed the corpse quite to the church; where, though I could not hear, I was informed that the dear minister* gave a very pathetic and instructive exhortation to the bystanders, as well as to the relatives. Oh, that I could say, it had the desired effect on my dear children! At present, alas! it is quite the reverse. But who can tell? Perhaps some precious soul

---

* The Rev. J. B—n, then Vicar of Olney.

might then be awakened, and in the Lord's due time brought to the knowledge of the truth; though we may never be ascertained of it, till our happy spirits meet in the world of glory. I now thought this world had no charms for me; but that I could, as it were, sit loose to all things here below: and I was so highly favoured of my adorable Saviour, that I trust I am not deceiving myself, when I say, I had many tokens of his love, to bear me up.

CONCLUSION.

THE abruptness with which the preceding narrative closes, is likely to disappoint the reader's expectations, in proportion to the degree in which the perusal may have interested his feelings. Endeavours have, therefore, been used to supply the deficiency, by inquiries among her family and neighbours: and various particulars have been collected; which, though incompetent to form a connected account of her latter years, may yet be useful, to explain several previous occurrences, and to satisfy the reader, that the close of her life was consistent with its tenor from the time of her conversion, and with the principles to which, in the foregoing sheets, she attributes the change of her conduct.

Christianity affords us no ground to suppose that its sincerest professors will be exempted from earthly afflictions: but it encourages us to seek for solid support and consolation under trials, and for a happy result from them, in our everlasting advantage. It leads us also to apprehend, that those objects which most powerfully attract our affections, however innocently, in this world, are likely to become the most copious sources of our distress. Such was the experience of Mary Saxby. The intelligent reader may have observed from the artless detail which she has given, that, amidst all her outward disadvantages, she possessed, in no common degree, what is usually termed strength of mind. With intellectual powers superior to her abject station, she was impelled by passions equally energetic, and was agitated by the most pungent sensibilities. No mother could more ardently love her offspring: no christian could more fervently desire their spiritual welfare. After having borne ten children, she was left with four daughters, at the death of their brother, as related above. Mary could scarcely be comforted for those which " were not;" yet she had to suffer more on account of her surviving family. As these will frequently be referred to in what remains to be added, it seems proper to introduce this sequel with some remarks on the state of her family from its commencement; especially as she has not mentioned, either the births, or the deaths, of her children, except they were attended with some remarkable circumstances.

The eldest daughter *Katherine,* was born at Woburn in 1762, when her mother was twenty-four years of age; and she is still living. The second child, *William,* born in 1765, was the lad who died at Stony Stratford, in his seventeenth year, about twelve months before his father. He had been apprenticed to his uncle, Spire Holloway,*

---

* The name was spelt *Hollowell* in the preceding notes, because it was thus entered in the church register of Mary's marriage at Olney. It is here altered, in consequence of information that her relations in London spell it in this manner.

in London, as a silk weaver, but had deserted him; and an invitation for him to return, did not arrive till after his sudden decease. A daughter, *Frances*, born in 1767, was always sickly; and died in 1769, soon after the birth of her next sister, *Keren-happuch*, who still survives. Her mother, although then living in wickedness, discovered some trace of her religious education, by an earnest wish to have her children called by scripture names. Accordingly, having consented, with some reluctance, that the first three should be named after the relations of John Saxby, she prevailed with him to let her next daughters be called after those of Job. The twins, of which she was delivered at Bradwin, in October 1772, were, therefore, named *Kezia*, and *Jemima*. The former died soon afterwards: the latter was burned to death in August 1774, near Wollaston in Northamptonshire, as related, p. 25. Another daughter, born in that year at Rushden, in the same county, likewise named *Kezia*, is still living. *Thomas*, who was drowned, was born at Stony Stratford, in 1776; and was placed apprentice at Olney, in the twelfth year of his age. Her last children were twin-daughters, named *Jemima*, and *Pámela*, born at Stony Stratford in 1779; the former of whom died there, but the latter survived her brother, and was the only one that resided with her mother, at the time of his death. She had then entered on her sixteenth year; and she was so much terrified at that distressing

event, as to fall dangerously ill: but she recovered, after her mother had, on that account,
removed to another house. Kezia, who had
lately married a person of Olney, named Benjamin Ping, lived also in the town ; but he had already left her, having enlisted into the County
Militia. In addition to the troubles in which these
circumstances involved their mother, she heard,
the very day after her son's death, that her eldest
daughter had destroyed herself at a neighbouring
village. This report, however, was happily found
to be a mistake ; having arisen from the dreadful
catastrophe of another vagrant woman. Katherine
had then a second husband, who was a soldier in
the army. During his absence, she travelled, as
her mother had formerly done, without any settled abode ; and being on the spot where the sui-
cide was committed by a woman of the same description, it was erroneously imputed to her. She
arrived, however, at Olney, seasonably to abridge
her mother's anguish on the account.

In the following winter, which was extremely
severe, Mary had to sympathize with her daughter Kezia, who was destitute of support, when she
was delivered of a child that shortly died ; but
the assistance of her mother's friends seasonably
alleviated her distress. Mary's affliction on this
account was exceeded by that which she sustained
in the following spring : when her youngest
daughter was seduced ; and instead of manifesting
repentance of her misconduct, addicted herself to

licentious courses. In May 1796, she entirely forsook her mother, to accompany a party of soldiers; and Mary in vain sent after her, to prevail on her to return. She came back, about six weeks afterwards, in a miserable condition; and being seized with a disorder that rendered her lame, was taken into the parish workhouse at Stony Stratford. It pleased God that she recovered, and returned to Olney; where she remained with Kezia, till the following Christmas. Their eldest sister being then a servant in the General Infirmary at Northampton (where she had previously been received as a patient), Pamela went to live in that town; but relapsing into vice, she became pregnant by a soldier, and returning to the workhouse at Stratford, was delivered of a dead child. After abiding at times with her mother, and affording her transient hopes of reformation, she went to Plymouth, in September 1799, with a soldier and his wife, with the latter of whom she had become intimately acquainted: and Mary remained, several months, in anxious suspense concerning her. In April 1800, she was married, at that place, to a sailor; and after visiting her mother during the summer, returned to Plymouth, accompanied by her sister Kezia.

While she had lived with her mother, Pamela usually went with her on the journeys which she took, in order to get her bread by selling trifling articles of drapery and haberdasher's goods. They travelled in three different directions, in North-

H

amptonshire, Buckinghamshire, and Bedfordshire, and Mary, being every where highly esteemed, was received with hospitality, and encouraged in her business, by pious people, whether Church folks, Methodists, or Dissenters. The writer of this brief account well remembers her deep distress on account of her youngest daughter's repeated misconduct; and the fond hopes which she indulged respecting her, whenever there appeared room to suppose that she was convinced of her guilt, and desirous of amendment. Pamela was born about the time of her mother's conversion; and of course had not been led to evil by her example. In their journeys together, she certainly had more opportunity of seeing good than evil. But such is the "desperate wickedness" of the human heart, that it is not uncommon, to observe young people depraved, notwithstanding the best means of advancement in religion and virtue. Let them who consider the mind of a child as blank paper, on which good or evil may be inscribed with equal facility, account for so obvious and so stubborn a fact!

This girl, whose welfare naturally lay with peculiar weight on her mother's mind, was by no means the sole occasion of her distress. It is well known, that the labouring and poorest classes of society in England, subsist almost wholly on bread; and that successive deficiencies of the harvests about ten years since, aggravated by the rapacity of capital farmers and dealers in corn, de-

prived innumerable families of the necessaries of
life. The measures which were taken by the
government for their supply, were frustrated,
partly by the artifices of interested people, and
partly by the wretched quality of the corn that was
abundantly imported. In general, the starving
poor sustained their miseries with the most laudable patience; but in such circumstances, it was
to be expected, that they would at times seize, and
appropriate to their perishing families, the loads
of corn which they saw removing, they knew not
whither. Women, as being more immediately
affected by the wants of their children, and less
liable than their husbands to the severity of the
law, were principal actors in riots of this nature :
and one of Mary's daughters exposed herself, in
this manner, to disgraceful punishment. Another, whose husband had long been unheard of,
grieved her mother by marrying again, before her
widowhood was certified. But Mary's distresses
were then approaching to their crisis, and to their
termination. The Father of mercies, who never
willingly afflicts his children, doubtless saw that
all her trials were necessary, to ripen her for a
state of endless happiness and honour; and removed her, amidst consoling circumstances, as
soon as she was " made meet for an inheritance
with his saints in light."

Her youngest daughter, though not abandoned
to vice after her marriage equally as before, continued to be, in various respects, an immoral

character. Like multitudes of the poor, previous to the introduction of vaccine inoculation, she had not been inoculated in childhood, with the small-pox; and she was attacked by this disorder at Plymouth in the summer of 1801. It proved severe and fatal; but its progress not being rapid, she had time to afford every proof of contrition, and repentance of her sinful course, that her situation could admit; and she died in hope of that mercy, which, in a few instances, has been vouchsafed (as some have observed) at the eleventh hour of the day; or rather, as the late Mr. Berridge once said, in reference to the thief on the cross, "just before the clock struck twelve!"

The validity of such a repentance can only be decided by infinite wisdom. It did not afford Mary effectual consolation, under this new affliction. She had long struggled with a very painful disorder; and she was then advancing in years, oppressed with the effects of youthful follies, and their attendant hardships. On receiving the news of Pamela's death, she was attacked by sudden and violent fits of asthma, which resulted in a rapid dropsy; complaints, that she had never before experienced. Kezia, returning to Olney after her sister's burial, found her mother in a dangerous state. Her husband, Benjamin Ping, had been there, on furlough from his regiment, while she was at Plymouth; and had resented her absence so strongly, that he vowed to murder her, if he ever saw her again. During the short time

which they at first spent together, they were unhappy; and while absent with the county militia,
he had never contributed to her support. As he
was expected soon to return to Olney, his wife
was on the point of quitting the place, to avoid
meeting him; when she received an affectionate
letter from him at Chelmsford, and soon afterwards another, which stated that he had been excited to a concern for his salvation, by the example and conversation of a fellow-soldier, who was
a native of Daventry, in Northamptonshire.
Keren-happuch, whose husband had been drawn
for the militia, accompanied him to the regiment; and coming at this time from Chelmsford,
to see her mother, confirmed the substance of
these letters. Mary rejoiced greatly at it, amidst
her sufferings; and exclaimed, " Lord! now
lettest thou thy servant depart in peace, for mine
eyes have seen thy salvation."

With the same disposition that is manifested by
her narrative, she expressed a confidence that she
should not die, before she had once more seen
him whom she now called " her Benjamin."
This expectation was gratified: he arrived on the
same day with her daughter Katherine, a few
weeks before her death; and remained with her
till its near approach, affording satisfactory evidence of the change which had taken place in his
heart. He attended on Mary with all the tenderness of an affectionate child; and usually ad-
ministered to her whatever nourishment she re-

ceived. Her asthmatic fits were so violent, that she was frequently expected to die in them; and she commonly remained insensible some time after they subsided. On recovering from one of these, she said to him (in allusion to his recent services in Ireland), "Benjamin, you have fought well for your king and country, and it was in a good cause: but now I hope you will fight in a still better cause. Fight, till you gain the victory, and win the prize of eternal glory." Being obliged to set out to join his regiment the next morning, she wished him the Lord's presence; expressed her hope to meet him in a better world; and said that she could then die in comfort respecting her daughter; for whom she should have been greatly distressed, but for the change which had passed on him.

She had never been able to go out of the house more than once, after hearing of Pamela's death: and she was so feeble that Kezia, who alone attended her till the arrival of her sisters, was obliged to carry her up and down the stairs. At length, she was wholly confined to her bed room; and her body began to mortify before her death. While it was practicable, notwithstanding interruptions from her asthmatic complaint, she maintained family prayer with her daughters. Her devotional language was remarkably fluent and expressive, but perfectly plain and unaffected. She often exhorted them not to trust to the prospect of repentance on a death-bed; urging how unfit she must have been for so solemn a work, if she had till then been a stranger to religion. Her complicated diseases, indeed, frequently deprived her of the command of her thoughts; and the natural impatience of her disposition then prevailed: but when capable of recollection, she appeared to be almost incessantly engaged in prayer. She expressed, throughout her illness, a humble, but confident persuasion, of the happiness of that state to which she was daily and sensibly hastening : but she was impressed, at times, with dread of the pangs of death ; chiefly from the impossibility of conceiving what they might prove. When she could no longer be moved from her bed, she said, " Well, I shall ere long be adorned with a glorious robe; and then . . . ." As she paused, one of her daughters said, " What then, mother ?"—" Then," she replied, " I shall be with Christ, and like him; which I have so long wished to be : but," she added, " I fear it will not be yet."

Her final deliverance, however, was protracted only two days later. On the Saturday evening, her pastor, Mr. H—ll—d, called to see her; as he, and many other friends, had often done, in her sickness. She was scarcely sensible; and some verses which she repeated, were not intelligible. During the night, she became incapable of taking any nourishment: and she remained silent; but was observed to continue in prayer, till about forty minutes before her death ; which occurred at noon, on Sunday, December 20, 1801. Thus, a wish which she had often intimated, to exchange an earthly sabbath for a heavenly one, was literally fulfilled, and earlier than she had expected. Her fears of the last struggle seemed to be previously removed; and they were not realised by any apparent symptom of pain. She was buried, two days afterwards, in the church-yard, by the side of her beloved son. The Rev. Mr. St—ns—n, vicar of Olney, who had frequently seen her during her illness, committed her to the grave; whither her corpse was attended by nearly all the members of the religious society with which she was immediately connected. Her pastor preached a discourse, that evening, from a text which she had chosen for the purpose: " As for me, I will behold thy face in righteousness; I shall be satisfied, when I awake, with thy likeness." Ps. xvii. 15.

The esteem with which she was universally regarded, precluded her want of any earthly support or comfort, that she could enjoy during her tedious and painful confinement: but she had a superior consolation, the only one, indeed, which was adequate to the severity of her trials, in a humble, but assured hope, of everlasting salvation, through faith in " the redemption that is in Jesus Christ." Some instruction in the gospel, we have seen, that she received in early childhood; and the impression which she retained from it, though insufficient to prevent her from making a dreadful progress in wickedness, yet appears to have occasionally checked her course, and to have preserved her from total ruin. Nothing, however, but a radical change of principles and affections, was likely to have recovered her from the depth of depravity to which she sunk; and nothing less can, in any case, be an effectual preparation for a future state of perfect holiness and felicity. Of this change, her conduct, for the last twenty-three years, afforded the clearest proof, and very salutary effects. She had the happiness, amidst all her troubles, of seeing several among those who were most dear to her, brought to the fear of God; and her example and conversation were useful far beyond the precincts of her immediate neighbourhood. During her latter years, she zealously availed herself of the cheap publications of short religious tracts, for the purpose of doing good, while performing her usual journeys; and when she had sold a number sufficient to replace their cost, she used to give the rest to persons who could not buy them. In several instances, her exertions are known to have succeeded, for the instruction of the ignorant, and the conversion of the profligate, and they probably were successful in many more than have been ascertained. It is, however, *example* alone, that is *certain* of doing any good. Hers was, happily, during her life, of extensive use; from the necessity she was under, of travelling frequently, and in various directions; and from the access which she gained, in her way of business, to those classes of society which are least familiar with means of instruction. In this view, and in others, her death was a loss, of greater importance than can easily be conceived by persons who were not acquainted with her: and the consideration may serve as an encouragement and an admonition to the well-disposed poor, against a supposition, that the sphere in which they are placed by the providence of God, excludes them from usefulness. May his blessing attend this publication; by which, " being dead, she yet speaks;" that the utility of the pattern which she exhibited, through the grace of God, may become more enlarged and effectual, than her personal efforts, zealous as they were, could ever have rendered it!

FINIS,

MORRIS,
Printer, Dunstable.

www.ingramcontent.com/pod-product-compliance
Lightning Source LLC
Chambersburg PA
CBHW081518040426
42447CB00013B/3263